Cactus

Madelaine Nunn

CURRENCY PRESS
The performing arts publisher

CURRENT THEATRE SERIES

First published in 2023
by Currency Press
Gadigal Land, PO Box 2287 Strawberry Hills, NSW, 2012, Australia
enquiries@currency.com.au
www.currency.com.au
in association with La Mama

Copyright: *Cactus* © Madelaine Nunn, 2023.

COPYING FOR EDUCATIONAL PURPOSES

The Australian *Copyright Act 1968* [Act] allows a maximum of one chapter or 10% of this book, whichever is the greater, to be copied by any educational institution for its educational purposes provided that that educational institution [or the body that administers it] has given a remuneration notice to Copyright Agency [CA] under the Act.

For details of the CA licence for educational institutions contact CA, 12 / 66 Goulburn Street, Sydney, NSW, 2000; tel: within Australia 1800 066 844 toll free; outside Australia 61 2 9394 7600; fax: 61 2 9394 7601; email: memberservices@copyright.com.au

COPYING FOR OTHER PURPOSES

Except as permitted under the Act, for example a fair dealing for the purposes of study, research, criticism or review, no part of this book may be reproduced, stored in a retrieval system, or transmitted in any form or by any means without prior written permission. All enquiries should be made to the publisher at the address above.

Any performance or public reading of *Cactus* is forbidden unless a licence has been received from the author or the author's agent. The purchase of this book in no way gives the purchaser the right to perform the play in public, whether by means of a staged production or a reading. All applications for public performance should be addressed to the author c / –Currency Press at the address above.

Typeset by Brighton Gray for Currency Press.
Cover image by Darren Gill. Cover features by Samuel Baulch.

Currency Press acknowledges the Traditional Owners of the Country on which we live and work. We pay our respects to all Aboriginal and Torres Strait Islander Elders, past and present.

 A catalogue record for this book is available from the National Library of Australia

Contents

CACTUS 1

Theatre Program at the end of the playtext

Cactus was first produced by La Mama at La Mama Courthouse Theatre, Melbourne, on the 24 June 2021, with the following cast:

ABBIE	Ayesha Harris-Westman
PB	Lucy Rossen

Director, Katie Cawthorne
Dramaturg, Jane FitzGerald
Lighting Designer, Aedan Gale
Sound Designer, Danni Esposito
Sound Assistant, Rachel Stone
Stage Manager, Claudia Howarth
Operator, August Shearman
Set Construction, Thomas Pidd
Set Dresser, Alex Donnelly
Producer, Madelaine Nunn

CHARACTERS

ABBIE, 17 years old
PB, 17 years old

MUM
DOCTOR
ANAESTHETIST
LEADER
WOMAN 1
WOMAN 2
WOMAN 3
LACHIE
KEVIN

SETTING

The action of the play takes place over the last year of high school, traversing time and place. The staging should be abstract rather than mimetic or naturalistic.

The 'not-quite-real' world moments should be consistent in imagery and soundscape.

NOTES

In the first production of *Cactus*, the actor playing PB personified all the other characters. It is also possible to have a larger cast. The scenes with other characters shouldn't be staged as naturalism.

The delivery of the text messages is up to the director. In the first production of *Cactus* they were voiced by the actors.

I encourage the producer to collaborate with artists from diverse backgrounds in the realisation and presentation of this work.

The play should move at a fairly fast clip.

A slash / indicates when the next person should start speaking.

A dash— indicates an interruption.

ABBIE and PB are in a world full of adults. It's not quite theirs yet.

This play text went to press before the end of rehearsals and may differ from the play as performed.

SCENE ONE

The 'not-quite-real' world.

Obscured by an omnipresent fog while ash-like spores drift through the air. This is a place sort of like real life only darker and colder. In the dark we hear the crackling of electricity and the low groan of thunder. It's disconcerting and all encompassing.

The sky strobes to reveal ABBIE, *alone.*

The storm subsides and the sun comes out.

ABBIE: There they are. The three of them and their dog. In their matching hats. Sitting on a tartan picnic blanket. NO! *Polka dot.* They're sitting on a *polka dot* picnic blanket under the dappled sunlight of a tree. Their very own Garden of Eden. The woman smiles to herself as she admires the day, as she admires her little bundle of joy crawling ... not crawling, *walking. Walking* across the blanket, arms outstretched and giggling. And as the child falls into her lap, a breeze brushes past her neck and sends a sharp shiver down her spine, but just before it can make her cold it's quickly warmed away by the sun and the touch of a hand. The man she sits next to puts his hands on her small feet and kisses her neck. She looks at him, he looks at her and they are a *picture of happiness*. A picture of love. A love you can taste like soft cheese or burnt marshmallows. A sticky love. A tender love. Love that makes love jealous. Love like a hot bath full of ...

    A school bell.

SCENE TWO

A high-school bathroom. It's stark.

ABBIE *is alone in a cubicle. The only light should be on* ABBIE, *it should feel narrow and confined.*

ABBIE *has her period ... great.*

ABBIE: Blood.
    Everywhere.

No-one told me it would happen like this.
No-one told me it would be this sticky.
Or this clumpy.
Or this wet!
It'll just be a few spots.
It'll be slow.
You'll feel it.
Well, I didn't!
And now it's everywhere.
I look around.
A tampon wrapper on the floor.
A purple hairband.
The bin.
The *electronic* bin in the corner of the cubicle.
It's blinking.
Its lid's ajar, kept open by half a pad sticking out the top.
I mean, it doesn't look *that* ... used.
I *guess* I could ...
NO!!
What am I doing?!
TOILET PAPER!
Toilet paper is your friend.
Ergh.
My undies will never be the same again.
Tiny little elephants that were once grey are now red.
No!
Not red, *brown red*.
It's even on my thighs.
I try to rub the blood off with paper, but it just sticks to my skin.
Toilet paper stuck to the blood on my fingertips.
I wish I didn't chew my nails.
I try to pick it off.
It rips.
I make it worse.
WHY is this toilet paper so thin?!
I bet you they buy it in bulk because it's cheaper.

I look up.
Not sure why? For guidance? For God.
Help me God! Why did you do this?!
I used to think God was a woman.
Now I know: *God is a man.*
An *evil* man.
Probably bald.
I open my eyes.
No God, just a ball of wet toilet paper stuck to the ceiling.
Ready to drop at any second.
I pull up my undies.
They're wet, it's gross.
I feel gross.
I quickly turn my skirt around.
The back now facing the side.
At least if there's blood on my hip, I can say I ran into the corner of a table.
A very *sharp* table.
Everyone can relate to that.
I quickly check my reflection in my phone.
My face as red as a beetroot.
Which I think is funny because I feel like I have no blood left in my body to make my face red, but anyway.

   She turns to the toilet bowl.

OH MY GOD?!!
I catch a glimpse of the toilet bowl.
That came out of *me*?!
If you murdered someone in the girls' toilets and then didn't bother to clean up, no-one would know the difference.
Thank God I'm alone.

   ABBIE *flushes the toilet.*

PB: Excuse me.

   A light reveals PB *on the toilet. It's a mirror image to that of* ABBIE.

   ABBIE *freezes.*

ABBIE: …
PB: Hello?
ABBIE: …
PB: Are you still there?
ABBIE: …
PB: I can see your feet.
ABBIE: Sorry. I, um, didn't hear you.
PB: Who is it?
ABBIE: Why?
PB: What?
ABBIE: It's Abbie.
PB: Abbie … ?
ABBIE: … Roberts.
PB: Abbie Roberts! I know you! You seem nice. You seem like a nice person who would do me a huge favour even though it's kind of gross and embarrassing and I'm sorry I even have to ask.
ABBIE: Okay?
PB: I … *unexpectedly* got my—
ABBIE: Yep.
PB: And I don't have any—
ABBIE: Yep.
PB: And my cubicle just ran out of—
ABBIE: Yep.

>ABBIE *hands a roll of toilet paper under the wall.*

>You need a lot, it's thin.

>*School bell.*

SCENE THREE

The oval. A bell goes. ABBIE *and* PB *lie on the grass, looking through a book.*

ABBIE: Physiotherapy? You get to wear runners all day.
PB: True. But what if you had to massage a hairy old man that has heaps of moles or like a skin infection or an *oozing wound*!
ABBIE: You don't have to massage people with oozing wounds. And if you do, they'd let you wear gloves.

PB: Dentistry? Cleaning teeth would be *so* satisfying. And people are so vulnerable.
ABBIE: But imagine how many times you'd get bitten—what about psychology? No gross body parts.
PB: It's basically being paid to people-watch and gossip. AND under an alias you could write a best-selling book based on the juicy lives of all your patients.
ABBIE: But what if one of the patients gets attached. And then they get your number. And then they emotionally blackmail you to speak to them, even if you're on a holiday, because if you don't, they'll kill themselves.
PB: Okay. That's fucked. I give up.
ABBIE: What does *follow your passion* even mean? Follow something you have intense emotion about?
PB: I think they say, *follow your curiosity*.
ABBIE: Mr Lee was like, '*Look at what your community needs and then fill that hole*'.
PB: He can fill *my* hole.
ABBIE: Eww.
PB: The whole system is fucked anyway. Like we're about to hit our peak and all they want us to think about is some dumb job. It's so stupid, think about it: we have a careers advisor. She's literally a *careers advisor*. That is her *career*. How can she be qualified to help anyone else unless they wanted to be a careers advisor? Makes no sense.
ABBIE: I guess she *knows how* to look at our skill set and interests and then *transfers them* into a professional context …

    PB *gives her a blank look.*

But yeah, you're so right, it's so stupid. I wish we could just fast-forward to when we're living in Berlin.
PB: And we have a short-haired sausage dog called Pepper.
ABBIE: And he's allowed inside.
PB: And we can have gin and tonics whenever we want.
ABBIE: Eww, I hate gin.
PB: Whatever! Vodka sodas whenever we want.
ABBIE: And I'll finally pull off red lipstick.
PB: And we have a combined net worth of five million dollars.

ABBIE: And our own clothing line.
PB: And a Vespa.
ABBIE: Two Vespas.
PB: Three Vespas.
ABBIE: Yes! And we can finally stop wearing—ouch.

> ABBIE *gets a stabbing pain deep inside her. She clutches her side.*

PB: You okay?
ABBIE: We can finally stop wearing maroon.
PB: Yes! A hundred and twenty days, that's all we have left. Not including weekends.
ABBIE: Easy.

> *School bell.*

SCENE FOUR

The library. ABBIE*'s head is slumped on top of a textbook. The sound of a bell.* PB *enters and sits across from* ABBIE.

PB: [*whispering*] Pssst!

> ABBIE *looks up.*

Did you hear about Jack Richards?
ABBIE: No.
PB: Okay, this is going to make you feel so much better.
ABBIE: What?
PB: Jack Richards got his dick *stuck in a test tube*.

> ABBIE *bolts upright.*

ABBIE: OH MY GOD?!
PB: Shhh. He put his dick in a glass test tube *AND THEN* his dick expanded so his skin suctioned tight to the walls of the test tube *AND THEN* it went purple *AND THEN* he had to waddle all the way from level one to the science staff room to tell Miss Hall that he needed to go to the hospital because the test tube was like *suffocating his dick*!
ABBIE: Did you see it?
PB: I wish! He was *bragging* about it when I walked past sick bay looking for you. He's not even smart enough to be embarrassed!

ABBIE: He's so dumb. Imagine if it shattered.
PB: Imagine if he got a boner while it was in there and it shattered on his dick.
ABBIE: He'd never be able to use it again. That's totally the natural selection gene aborting itself.
PB: How do you think they got it off?
ABBIE: Maybe they slipped it off with oil or cream.
PB: Like when a ring gets stuck on your finger.
ABBIE: He'd probably enjoy that though.
PB: Hopefully they poured cold water on it or dipped it in a bucket of ice as punishment. To make it *shrivel* back into his body.
ABBIE: Eww, shrivelled dick.
PB: I am SO glad I don't have a dick.
ABBIE: Really? But think of all the things you can put it in. Like test tubes.

SCENE FIVE

Behind the school oval. ABBIE *is reading the back of a Panadol packet.* PB *is pacing.*

PB: Ninety-two.
ABBIE: Huh?
PB: Days left. Not including weekends.
ABBIE: Hey, what do you think would actually happen if I took three Panadols at once?
PB: I dunno. Not much.
ABBIE: What about four?
PB: It's probably fine. They make the pills bigger than they need to be as a way to trick people into thinking they're taking more than they actually are so they're less likely to overdose.
ABBIE: Really?
PB: It's a placebo thing.
ABBIE: So four at once would be fine?
PB: Probably. When you think about it, ninety-two days isn't actually that long. I just hope I'm still not a virgin by the end of it.
ABBIE: Is five pushing it?
PB: Five's pushing it. Do you think Jez has done it yet?
ABBIE: I don't think so. How many hours has it been since maths?

PB: Like three and a half. I don't think we're ugly, there are definitely uglier girls than us, right?
ABBIE: Yeah. We're mid-range. It's okay to take Panadol with Coke, right?
PB: I think so. I wonder if Jez knows that I love him? God he's so handsome, he's like a walking crème brûlée.
ABBIE: If I give you money will you get me a Coke?
PB: If I get you a Coke, will you tell me what's going on?
ABBIE: Nothing's going on.
PB: It's happening again, isn't it?
ABBIE: No.
PB: Tell me.
ABBIE: I'm just thirsty.
PB: It is.
ABBIE: Only a little bit.
PB: You need to tell someone!
ABBIE: You need to buy me a Coke.
PB: Fine. If I buy you a Coke you have to talk to Jez about me.
ABBIE: Fine.

> As PB *leaves the sun drifts behind the clouds and the colour fades from the sky. The world shifts.*
>
> ABBIE *looks up and notices something in the distance. There is a crackling of electricity and the low groan of thunder.*
>
> PB *enters and it snaps* ABBIE *back.*

PB: Did you want Diet, Zero or normal?
ABBIE: Normal.

> *Blackout.*

SCENE SIX

The dressing room of an op shop. PB *and* ABBIE *are admiring themselves in a mirror. They are wearing big fur coats and sunglasses.*

ABBIE: I love it!
PB: I love it!
ABBIE: You look incredible!
PB: You look incredible!

ABBIE: Really?
PB: Yes!
ABBIE: Be honest. Do you actually think I can pull it off?
PB: Is that even a question?
ABBIE: Yes.
PB: Yes. You can pull it off. It's like this was made for you.

    ABBIE *sniffs the inside of the coat.*

ABBIE: It smells weird. Like the skin from the previous owner is still stuck to the inside.
PB: That's authenticity!
ABBIE: Wait. Do you think this is real?
PB: Probably.
ABBIE: I think they're real.
PB: What do you expect?
ABBIE: I don't know if I can—
PB: Don't!
ABBIE: Don't you think it's a little weird that this was once a living creature and now it just hangs off a coat hanger.
PB: We didn't kill it.
ABBIE: I know but it's—
PB: What do you think the wolf would do if it saw us in the wild? We're the animals on top, it's natural.
ABBIE: I hate when people say that.
PB: It's natural?
ABBIE: We're animals.
PB: We have instincts and urges, primal *SEXUAL urges*.

    PB *starts playfully humping* ABBIE, *making sexual noises as she humps.*

ABBIE: Shhh!! They're going to think that we're shoplifting.
PB: You know how to stop them thinking that?
    By buying the coat!
ABBIE: I like it, I really like it. I think it's cool, I just don't think I'm cool enough to wear it.
PB: C'mon, Abbie!
ABBIE: I'm going to sweat my tits off in this.
PB: Beauty is pain and besides, you look like you know what you stand for.

ABBIE: I don't know what I stand for.
PB: It *looks* like you do! You exude confidence, you radiate presence, you embody elegance.
ABBIE: You're just saying words now.
PB: Good words.
ABBIE: It's four-thirty and we haven't even looked at dresses.
PB: Oh my God.
ABBIE: What?
PB: Oh my God.
ABBIE: What?!
PB: I just had the best idea, I'm the smartest person in the entire world.

> PB *pauses for dramatic effect.*

We should wear these to formal!!

> PB *strikes a pose.*

ABBIE: These?
PB: How cool would that be?
Undeniably cool. Admit it! We would be unstoppable in these.
ABBIE: You don't think people will think we look like …

> ABBIE *is hit with a deep pain. The world slightly darkens.*

PB: … Babes? Yes.
Anyway, who cares! It'll probably be the last time we ever see these fuckers. Let's make a mark. Leave a lasting impression.

> ABBIE *comes back into the world.*

ABBIE: I don't think I can pull it off. You're good at standing out while blending in. I just want to blend in.

> ABBIE *takes off the coat and thrusts it towards* PB.

PB: Do you like the coat or not?
ABBIE: It doesn't matter.
PB: I'm checking the price.

> PB *walks off with the coats.*
>
> ABBIE *turns to check herself in the mirror, it's a lingering moment, she runs her eyes all over her body. The sky strobes slightly and the sound of electricity creeps in. There is a rumble.*
> ABBIE *looks up, she sees something out in front of her.*

SCENE SEVEN

Abbie's house. A guttural cry of pain. ABBIE *is curled up on the ground in a foetal position.* PB *is standing over her.*

PB: Breathe. Just breathe.
ABBIE: I must have been a cockroach in a past life. Or a Spartan. Or a VOODOO DOLL!
PB: Calm down!
ABBIE: Or even possibly Hitler—Oh my God! *I* was *Hitler*?!
PB: If you were Hitler, you'd be a cockroach in this life, not a woman.
ABBIE: I think a cockroach would be better.

    ABBIE *pushes out quick, sharp breaths.*

PB: You're going to make yourself hyperventilate!
ABBIE: Good! Then I'll pass out. Arghhhh!
PB: What's happening?
ABBIE: I'm going to vomit.
PB: Now?
ABBIE: OH NO!
PB: Where's a bucket?
ABBIE: Shit!
PB: What?!
ABBIE: I *need* to SHIT!
PB: Get up! Get up! Get up!
ABBIE: I can't move.
PB: You can't shit yourself.

    A moment of pause.

ABBIE: I think it's over.
PB: The pain?
ABBIE: Life!
PB: I'm calling your mum.
ABBIE: No! She'll just worry.
PB: Fine. I'll call an ambulance.
ABBIE: No. *Please—*
PB: You just told me you were dying!

ABBIE: I DUNNO! I could be but I dunno!
PB: Hey Siri. *SIRI!*

   PB's phone beeps in acknowledgement.

Can you die from period pain?
ABBIE: You believe in that, don't you?
PB: Dying?
ABBIE: Reincarnation.
PB: Of course, it makes the most sense.
ABBIE: Energy can't be destroyed nor created—
PB: Listen! [*Reading*] Although you feel that you are going to die because of the pain, it is highly unlikely that you will.
ABBIE: Unlikely?!
PB: *Highly* unlikely.
ABBIE: But there's still a chance? Is this death? Is this what death feels like?
PB: There's boobs all over this page, I don't trust it.
ABBIE: If I don't make it to formal tell—
PB: [*reading*] Can you die from period pain?
     Anne Smith says: 'No, I don't think so.'
     Thanks Anne.
ABBIE: Anne you bitch!
PB: Glenn Samson says: 'No, not to date.'
ABBIE: Fuck you, Glenn! What would you know?!
PB: It says here he's a nurse—but who really fucking knows?!

   PB*'s scrolling through her phone.*

ABBIE: I kept stealing all of Claire Stewart's red pens even though she asked me to give them back!
PB: What kind of pain is it?
ABBIE: And in primary school I was mean to Ben Kaisak for no reason!
PB: Is it dull, throbbing, sharp—
ABBIE: Sharp! Like there's a … *cactus* inside me.

    ABBIE *and* PB *look at each other for a moment. Then* ABBIE *groans loudly.*

AHHHHHH—What does it say?!
PB: It just says this is normal.
ABBIE: How can this be (normal) —

PB: I dunno! This has never happened to me.
ABBIE: Don't tell me that!
PB: I don't even get cramps—
ABBIE: So I'm a freak and I'm dying!
PB: Maybe it's not even period pain, maybe it's something you ate or... or ... appendicitis!
ABBIE: I'll buy her new pens! UNIVERSE, ARE YOU LISTENING?! And I'll do something nice for Ben Kaisak. Please!!
PB: Maybe you need to do a really big fart!
ABBIE: Fuck you.
PB: I'm serious! It happened to this guy on *Mystery Diagnosis*!

    ABBIE *starts to sob.*

    PB *starts to call someone.*

Hi Mrs Roberts, it's PB here. I'm good, thank you. I think you need to come home.

SCENE EIGHT

The beach car park. ABBIE *and* PB *are sitting on the hood of PB's car.* ABBIE *is trying to get a rock out of her shoe with a stick.* PB *is eating gummy bears.*

ABBIE: Uncomfortable?
PB: So it didn't feel good at all?
ABBIE: You're sick.
PB: It's a legit question!
ABBIE: No.
PB: That's disappointing. Who was your nurse?
ABBIE: Why?
PB: It's important.
ABBIE: It was an old, unimpressed Eastern European lady who stunk of cigarettes.
PB: She's probably unsatisfied herself, doesn't know how to yield pleasure.
ABBIE: It's not her job to *yield pleasure*.
PB: Maybe if it was a cute grad, fresh out of uni. That might have made the experience a little more memorable.
ABBIE: Trust me. It's memorable.
PB: How big are we talking?

    PB *is measuring with her hands getting bigger each time.*

This. This. THIS?!

ABBIE: You know my mum's decorative pepper grinder?

PB: The one she keeps in the glass cabinet?

ABBIE: It was as big as that, only metal.

PB: OH MY GOD—Did she put anything on it?!

ABBIE: Yeah, she was really nice. She actually drew a smiley face on it just before it went in.

PB: Really?

ABBIE: No! That would've been SO unhygienic and very disturbing.

PB: I mean, did she prepare you, was there anything in the room?

ABBIE: It's not a sperm clinic, there's no porn in the background!

PB: Like lube, did she use any lube?

ABBIE: She used like an entire bottle, she just kept squeezing it on. I even made a joke, I was like *'leave some for the others!'*

PB: Did she laugh?

ABBIE: No.

PB: Oh.

    Slight pause.

What brand of lube did she use?

ABBIE: I dunno? The *generic hospital* brand? You're obsessed.

PB: I'm just trying to get all the details.

ABBIE: I think she knew.

PB: What?

ABBIE: That I was a …

PB: Pisces? Atheist?

ABBIE: Virgin.

    ABBIE *throws the stick away.*

PB: She wouldn't know! These medical people barely pay attention to the actual patients. She was probably too busy fantasising about having a ciggie in the next break.

And besides, anyone would be tight in that situation.

ABBIE: Eww.

PB: Even Stacey Mulls would be tight in that situation and she's had more D than Mary Magdalene.

ABBIE: Mary Magdalene was wrongly accused.
PB: Was she?
ABBIE: Yes!

    ABBIE *covers her face in her hands.*

PB: Don't worry. Most girls cry the first time.
ABBIE: I didn't cry.
PB: Well you've still had more action than me.
ABBIE: That's not hard.

    PB *opens her mouth aghast!*

PB: Harsh but true. At least it's prepared you for sex.
ABBIE: With a robot!
PB: The future holds exciting possibilities.
    Gummy bear?

    PB *offers* ABBIE *the packet of gummy bears. She takes one.*

  So when exactly is the … procedure?
ABBIE: Two days.
PB: Two days?! Don't we have that English exam?
ABBIE: Special consideration, please and thank you.
PB: You're so lucky.
ABBIE: Not really. I do have to starve myself for an entire day.
PB: But is your surgeon hot?
ABBIE: She's kind of old but yeah? Sort of, for an older woman.
PB: Well, my cousin's boyfriend is an anaesthetist, and he is hands down the hottest person I've ever met, once I had to remove myself from his presence because I thought I was going to faint from his charisma. If he had even smiled at me, I would've cum on the floor. So hopefully you have *him*.
ABBIE: I just hope I don't have to share a room.
PB: I'll bring you earplugs, although I'm sure Leanne's already thought of them.
ABBIE: I think she has a whole first-aid kit, it's like, *Mum we're going to a hospital, they have these things.*
PB: Leanne's such a MILF.
ABBIE: Eww.
PB: It's a good thing. Means you're going to be a MILF too.

ABBIE: Your mum's pretty hot.

PB: But she's not motherly. If it was me, Mum would be like, *'Can you get your brother to take you?'*

ABBIE: Well, I'm pretty sure my dad thinks I'm getting my wisdom teeth removed.

PB: If it's the same thing my neighbour had, she said it's like, getting your insides carved out like you're a pumpkin on Halloween.

ABBIE: Why would you say that?!

PB: I'm SO SORRY. I don't know why I said that. But you can't feel it *obviously*. You just wake up after it's done and all the pain will be gone.

ABBIE: Unless I wake up conscious yet paralysed.

PB: That's not going to happen.

ABBIE: The morphine wears off but it's too late, the paralysis has set in and I'm just screaming on the inside but no-one can hear me. Trying to make a sign, a signal, to let them know I'm awake and that I can feel everything—

PB: That's not going to happen!

They keep one hand conscious so you can click if you wake up.

ABBIE: Maybe I'll say I'm heavier than what I actually am so they give me more morphine.

PB: Morphine is like hospital heroin.

ABBIE: Really?

PB: So unfair. Doing drugs and skipping English.

ABBIE: You'll be fine.

PB: So will you. And I'll be praying for you.

ABBIE: Since when do you / pray—

PB: Praying that a hot young grad is in your ward.

SCENE NINE

A hospital corridor. ABBIE *gets put into a hospital gown.*

Text messages: all in separate texts.

ABBIE: My gown is open at the back. I think everyone can see my butt.

PB: I always thought bleaching and waxing your butthole was stupid but hospitals should really offer it as a pre-surgery service because it's a violation.

PB: *But you should totally flaunt it.*
PB: *To all the cute grads.*
ANAESTHETIST: Lie down please.
ABBIE: Obviously PB's prayers didn't work. The anaesthetist is an old man with ear hair. I smile at him, don't know why, instinct, I guess. He doesn't smile back, just shoves the needle in and tapes it down. It hurts. Apparently, he's in charge of my vitals so if I die, he's the one responsible. In a sick way, I hope I do die to get back at him for being rough. But in a very normal way, I hope I don't.
DOCTOR: How are you feeling?
ABBIE: At least my doctor's nice.
DOCTOR: Do you understand what's going to happen?
ABBIE: Not really but for some reason I nod like I do. She smiles and then I'm off. I'm being wheeled down the corridor by my blue entourage. I pretend I'm famous and that I'm being led to side of stage.
DOCTOR: In here.
ABBIE: The next room is brighter. Sounds are louder. Faces are bigger. One of the nurses has her phone out showing another nurse a picture of her dog. I hope she washes her hands before she—
ANAESTHETIST: Alright here we go, count down from ten for me and you won't feel a thing.
ABBIE: Ten, nine, eight, fuck, seven, I'm still here, six, don't, five, cut, four, me op—

Blackout.

SCENE TEN

The 'not-quite-real' world. There is the low drone of thunder and the occasional crackle of electricity. ABBIE *appears standing with her eyes closed, almost floating. A sharp breath in and she wakes, alone.*

She looks down at her hands and then at her body.

She looks around trying to figure out where she is when her body is struck.

Different parts of her body begin to move outside of her control.

Each movement is isolated.

It builds and builds and then muted hospital noises infiltrate the space. The vibration of Abbie's phone starts to slowly remove her from this world. Text messages: all in separate texts.

MUM: *I'm just in the corridor talking to Dad.*
MUM: *Let me know when you wake up. LOL OF LOVE.*
MUM: *Whoops. Silly auto-correct. LOTS OF LOVE.*

SCENE ELEVEN

A hospital room. ABBIE, *in her gown, is sitting up in bed.* PB *is at the foot of the bed.*

PB: And then Kevin fingered Eliza in the bushes while he was still wearing all his rings.
ABBIE: I would die before letting Kevin and his ring fingers touch me.
PB: He definitely doesn't buy sterling silver, and cheap jewellery turns the ear skin green so imagine what it does to the vagina skin.
ABBIE: He probably gave her an STI!
PB: He probably created his own *strain* of STI!
ABBIE: Eww. Anything else?
PB: Ahh … Casey's dad tripped over while he was bringing out the spanakopita and tomato sauce went all over Jez. That was pretty funny. Casey's dad's hot too. He used to be a pro-surfer or like a world champion wind glider or something. Definitely a DILF. Umm … Oh! So you know how Greggie loves animals, well she desperately wanted to pat Casey's cow—I know, it's so weird, I don't even know if cows like to be petted, but yeah, anyway—so she went out the back but it was dark, the sensor light wasn't working and she's like the clumsiest person ever, so of course, there was a ditch, and of course she fell into the barbed-wire fence and tore a chunk out of her leg. We told her to pour alcohol on it, meaning vodka or something so she wouldn't get an infection, but she just poured a whole bottle of Midori on it instead.

> *Midori can be changed to a drink with the most relevance to young people. It should be something you don't want to pour on a wound.*

ABBIE: Ew, why was she drinking Midori?

PB: That's what I said!

ABBIE: Was it fun?

PB: Mildly. Awkward drive home though—pretending we were sober to Angie's mum at like four a.m.

ABBIE: I thought you said it wasn't fun.

PB: I only stayed that late because I was getting a lift home with Angie.

ABBIE: Oh. Who ended up going?

PB: Umm just the usuals. Lachie Latham ended up coming.

ABBIE: Really? What happened? Did anything happen? Did he talk to anyone—anyone in particular, like *who*, *who* did he talk to?

> PB *laughs.*

… What?

PB: You love him SO much.

ABBIE: No! I just was interested in why he, like what he, I just meant— shut up.

> ABBIE *is disappointed. She starts doing some tai chi-esque breathing movements.*

PB: I didn't talk to him. He just sat near the slushy machine and played on his phone.

[*Referring to the tai chi*] What are you doing?

ABBIE: I'm relaxing. I'm trying to connect my brain muscle with my vag muscle so I can finally pee.

PB: So you seriously can't feel *anything* below your belly button?

ABBIE: I can but I can't.

PB: So you basically have a phantom pussy?

ABBIE: Pretty much.

PB: So are you … better?

ABBIE: Yeah. Sort of.

PB: What do you mean sort of?

ABBIE: The pain is slowly going and the scars are meant to fade but apparently I can't have kids. Or something.

> *Small beat.*

PB: What?

ABBIE: I don't know. My ovaries were like twisted? And the tubes were like blocked or scarred or both. Apparently, I already had low fertility or whatever, so this has practically sealed the deal.
PB: Oh.
ABBIE: Yeah.
PB: That sucks.
ABBIE: Yeah.
PB: Could you get a second opinion?
ABBIE: Mum's already sent the scans and information to like five other doctors.
PB: So what are you going to do?
ABBIE: Nothing.
PB: Nothing?
ABBIE: What can I do?
PB: Couldn't you freeze your eggs or start eating fish?
ABBIE: Start eating fish?
PB: Omega-3! Like couldn't you start eating fertility increasing foods?
ABBIE: That's definitely pseudoscience.
PB: But we're in the twenty-first century. They would have technology to like, you know, help you have a child.
ABBIE: Oh my God.
PB: What?
ABBIE: The way we're talking about this. We're talking about it like it's—I don't want kids so it doesn't matter.
PB: Yeah, yeah, of course. Kids are cunts. And they legit eat your brain. Like baby brain is a real thing, the baby eats it. Eats your grey matter. That's why they don't let new mothers drive.

SCENE TWELVE

Abbie's house. MUM *and* ABBIE *are in the kitchen.*

ABBIE: Mum burns herself on the water washing up—she's about to swear but just bites her lip instead. She usually orders me to dry but tonight she doesn't, just tells me to—
MUM: Sit back and relax at the table.
ABBIE: Why does she always have to make things weird? She's facing the sink when she—

MUM: You know you can talk to me. I'm here whenever you need. It's a lot to process at such a young—
ABBIE: It must be hard for her. I remember as a kid asking her what she wanted for Christmas or for her birthday, thinking she'd say flowers or jewellery or a new handbag. But every time she'd say the same thing: Nothing, I've got you. The only gift I need.
MUM: And who knows what technology we might have in fifteen years. I think if we can inhabit Mars, we should be able to—
ABBIE: All the wonders of the world and she thinks *I'm* the best thing that's ever happened to her.
MUM: Did I tell you that Brian and Todd from down the road have been looking into adopting, now they've got the money. And Kara's sister—
ABBIE: I heard her crying in the shower last night. I just stood outside the door listening. I thought about going in and asking her if she was alright, but then I thought it was better to just pretend I didn't hear.
MUM: Oh! And just my luck, there was a special on at Coles, so there's cake and ice cream in the freezer. I got chocolate swirl, your favourite.

SCENE THIRTEEN

The school gym. PB *and* ABBIE *are standing in a fight position.*

PB: S stands for solar plexus. Guts.

> PB *shows her kneeing someone in the stomach.* ABBIE *copies.*

I is for instep. Foot.

> PB *shows her stomping the ground,* ABBIE *copies.*

N stands for—
ABBIE: Nose?
PB: Someone knows their anatomy.

> ABBIE *scrunches up her nose and makes a face at* PB. PB *shows her punching someone in the face,* ABBIE *copies.*

And G is for groin. Which is the—
ABBIE: I know what the groin is.

PB: The only time you should lift your leg high is for a hard kick in the dick.

> PB *shows her a kick straight up through the air,* ABBIE *copies.*

Do you need me to go through it again?

ABBIE: Nup.

PB: You can stop if you forget or need a break. Okay. Five, six, seven, eight—

> ABBIE *and* PB *do the routine together.*

BOTH: S stands for solar plexus.

I is for instep.

N stands for nose.

G is for groin!

S stands for solar plexus.

I is for Instep.

N stands for nose.

G is for groin!

> ABBIE *does it again even quicker. It should be evenly punctuated. She does the moves smoothly and efficiently like a kickboxer would.* PB *watches, impressed.*

ABBIE: S stands for solar plexus.

I is for instep.

N stands for nose.

G is for groin!

[*Knees*] Bang.

[*Steps*] Bang.

[*Punches*] Bang.

[*Kicks*] Bang!

[*Knees*] Bang.

[*Steps*] Bang.

[*Punches*] Bang.

[*Kicks*] Bang!

PB: And the attacker is dead!!

ABBIE: I feel like I can punch a bear!

PB: Ms Morgan is going to froth when she sees you doing this.

ABBIE: Good. Cos I'm pretty sure I just failed maths.

PB: I don't think you've ever failed anything.
ABBIE: Hopefully I get at least one point for writing my name.
PB: Don't you get special consideration?
ABBIE: I don't really need it.
PB: You missed school.
ABBIE: I didn't miss that much.
PB: Why would you not use it?
ABBIE: All I need to do is catch up.
PB: But if you can't—
ABBIE: And I'd have to fill out all the forms and then everyone would be like [*impersonating a douchebag guy*] 'Why do you get special treatment?'
PB: I can totally see Liam saying that.
ABBIE: And they'd make me sit in a different room with that chick who pulls her hair out.
PB: She only does that so she's given more time.
ABBIE: There'd still be some old exam supervisor breathing down my neck.
PB: What about extensions on assignments?
ABBIE: I dunno.
PB: You should totally use that for history.
ABBIE: Maybe.

The end-of-lunch bell goes.

PB: Ready to solar plex this shit?
ABBIE: I'm ready to kick it in the dick.

ABBIE *and* PB *high kick the air.*

SCENE FOURTEEN

The oval. ABBIE's *on her phone,* PB *is studying* Hamlet.

PB: Whether 'tis nobler in the mind to suffer …
　　Whether 'tis nobler in the mind to suffer …
　　Whether 'tis nobler in the mind to—
ABBIE: Did you know, Kylie Minogue has a net worth of a hundred and twenty million dollars?
PB: No I didn't.

Whether 'tis nobler in the mind to suffer
The slings and arrows of outrageous fortune
Something, something, something.

ABBIE: And Dolly Parton owns more than three hundred wigs! And she's a librarian, AND she sleeps in her make-up!

PB: Who?

ABBIE: Dolly Parton. She's like a famous country singer.

PB: Oh yeah. Miley's grandmother.

ABBIE: I think you mean godmother.

PB: Whatever. I'd die to be able to sleep in my make-up.
To die, to sleep ... Oh my God!
Do you know about the poo yet?

ABBIE: The poo?

PB: You know, the random poos that were turning up all over school.

ABBIE: Oh yeah, the ones from the ESL teacher's labrador?

PB: It wasn't the labrador.

ABBIE: What?

PB: Guess who was doing the poos all along.

Excitedly trying to guess like it's a game.

ABBIE: Umm! Umm! Oh! Caitlin Gregg!

PB: Guess again.

ABBIE: Umm umm.

PB: It's so obvious when you think about it.

ABBIE: Umm, I dunno! Tell me!

PB: Jack. Test Tube. Richards!

ABBIE: NO!

PB: YES! Apparently, when Mrs Kim was doing that interview about 'community engagement' or whatever, in the far background you can see him—Jack—squatting on the bubbler basin, pants around his ankles just, you know, doing it.

ABBIE: Doing it?

PB: *Pooing.*

ABBIE: In the bubbler?

PB: Amazing isn't it. Apparently, it's airing tonight and he's going to go viral.

ABBIE: I wonder if they'll blur his face.

PB: I wonder if they'll blur his butt.
ABBIE: It'll probably make him famous.
PB: I'd so watch him on *MAFS*.
ABBIE: Same!
PB: Or *Survivor*! Actually, he'd be *so good* on *Survivor*!

> MAFS *and* Survivor *can be changed to any current reality show.*

ABBIE: Speaking of survivors. Did you know Oprah was only nineteen when she started co-anchoring news? And Gloria Steinem, the lady who revolutionised feminism, only started school when she was eleven years old.
PB: Why are you fact-checking these people? Do we need to know this for something?
ABBIE: There's just so many influential women out there.
PB: Yeah.
ABBIE: And like a lot of them don't have kids.

> PB *looks up at* ABBIE.

ABBIE: Like a lot of people you think do, but don't. Like Jennifer Aniston, Marilyn Monroe—

> *The names of the celebrities without children can be changed to any celebrities currently in the zeitgeist.*

PB: Joan of Arc!
ABBIE: Joan of Arc?
PB: She's such an icon.
ABBIE: Yeah, but she was also burnt at the stake.
PB: Yeah, but she led an army. Oh my God, YOU could lead an army! You could be the next Joan of Arc! You could be our Prime Minister or like, head of the UN.
ABBIE: What?
PB: Think of all the things you're going to be able to do now!
ABBIE: What do you mean?
PB: I knew you were going to change the world the moment I met you. Now there's no excuse!
ABBIE: So now I'm expected to change the world because I won't have an excuse?
PB: No. Shit. No. That's not what I meant. I just thought—

ABBIE: That's not why I was looking that up— I was just impressed that lots of women *choose* not to have kids.
PB: Yeah, of course.
ABBIE: A lot of women actually regret having kids.
PB: Yeah.
ABBIE: And you might not be able to have them either, you just don't know it yet.
PB: Yeah, that's possible.
ABBIE: It's actually quite common.
PB: I know.
ABBIE: And it really doesn't matter.

SCENE FIFTEEN

A community hall. ABBIE *and her* MUM *sit in a circle with a group of other women.*

LEADER: I want everyone to know that we're in a triple-S.
    A Safe Supportive Space where everyone is—
ABBIE: Of course, we're in a circle. And of course, there's complimentary tea and coffee. No biscuits though. That's disappointing. The hall we're in is covered in shit finger paintings and weird craft that can only be made by children; I wonder if it's triggering for the other women.
LEADER: If you're ever feeling overwhelmed or just need a break, you're very welcome to take a moment in the—
ABBIE: Mum squeezes my leg. I think she realises coming here was a mistake. The first woman to speak is sitting across from me. She's wearing white sneakers and has perfectly shaved legs.
WOMAN 1: I found out I wasn't invited to the christening of my friend's newborn. I think it was her way of protecting my feelings. But it was hard not to feel hurt when I saw the photos on Facebook.
ABBIE: They all nod in unison. The next woman to speak is wearing tight black stilettos. Her skin is red on the edge where they rub.
WOMAN 2: When Gina, the intern, announced her pregnancy at work, I cried in the toilets for half an hour. Then I touched up my face and went straight to a meeting.
ABBIE: More nodding and humming. They talk about how their friends are always busy with their families, the unsolicited advice, the

constant looks of pity. How it's a deal-breaker for the 'good guys' and an asset for the 'shit guys'.
WOMAN 3: I never thought I wanted a baby but then one morning I woke up and I did. But I'd left it too late.
ABBIE: This is the fucking saddest, most depressing place I've ever been. I look up at Mum. She's got a tissue in her hand, holding back tears.
LEADER: Abbie?
ABBIE: Shit. It's my turn.

    I'll pass, thanks.

    ABBIE *looks up at the ceiling. There is the rumble of thunder.*

SCENE SIXTEEN

Abbie's room. ABBIE *is alone.*

Text messages: all in separate texts.

ABBIE: *Where are you?*

ABBIE: *Want to hang out?*

ABBIE: *Call me when you see this.*

ABBIE: *I've had the weirdest fucking evening and just want some chips.*

ABBIE: *Salty chips.*

ABBIE: *I know globalisation is bad but Maccas has a point on consistency.*

ABBIE: *I need chips and gummy bears. ASAP.*

ABBIE: *Peebs?*

ABBIE: *PEEBS?*

SCENE SEVENTEEN

The bus stop. ABBIE *is standing there alone when* PB *comes up behind her and smacks her on the ass.*

PB: Ask me what happened last night.
ABBIE: Why didn't you text me back?
PB: Ask me what happened last night?
ABBIE: Did you see my texts?

PB: I dropped my phone in the toilet, it's been in rice all day. Ask me what happened last night!
ABBIE: What happened last night?
PB: I did it!
ABBIE: What?!
PB: I had sex with a human penis!
ABBIE: Seriously?
PB: Am I glowing?
ABBIE: Who with?
PB: Jez.
ABBIE: At his house?
PB: At the beach. We were just hanging out having this really nice dinner and then one thing led to another and then it happened. It really happened.
ABBIE: What was it like?
PB: It was actually really romantic.
ABBIE: Really? What were you eating?
PB: Maccas. But the whole scene was romantic, not just the dinner. Like listening to the ocean waves and me cuddling up to him cos the breeze was kind of cold and I'd left my jacket in his car. We were just chatting and joking and then one minute I was holding a gherkin and the next minute I was holding a dick.
ABBIE: Oh my God!
PB: And then we were taken by the moment and then it was over and I wasn't a virgin anymore.
ABBIE: But it's what you wanted, right?
PB: SO what I wanted.
ABBIE: What about the sand?
PB: It was a bit grindy and a little chafe-y and I keep finding sand in *really* weird places. But it added to this raunchy lust we had going on, plus it was *so romantic*.
ABBIE: Did you use a … ?
PB: Yeah, he had a condom in his wallet that he'd been saving for me. *Strawberry*.
ABBIE: That's nice?
PB: SO nice.
ABBIE: Was it good?

PB: SO good! I mean, short but good.
ABBIE: The sex or his—?
PB: No, no the sex. His dick was big.
ABBIE: Did you use lube?
PB: No. But we didn't need it.
ABBIE: Wait. When you say short. How short?
PB: I don't know. It's hard to tell in the moment.
ABBIE: So when you touched it, what was it like?
PB: It was like … one of those fancy rice-paper rolls your mum gets. If you froze it and then half defrosted it, so it's hard in the middle but soft on the outside but still hard overall. And then you loosely wrapped it in another layer of *very soft*, *very warm* rice paper. And then imagine holding it in one hand and there's a little bit of clear sauce leaking out the top.
It's like that.
ABBIE: Right.
PB: I actually feel different now, I dunno, like something's been lifted from me.
ABBIE: Like what?
PB: I feel more connected to the rest of the world or something. Or just like more knowledgeable. But how are you?
ABBIE: Still a virgin.
PB: What did you text me about?
ABBIE: Doesn't matter. Just if you understood the maths homework.
PB: No fucking way.

SCENE EIGHTEEN

The 'not-quite-real' world. ABBIE.

ABBIE: There they are. The three of them. In their matching hats … No. *Jackets.* In their matching jackets. They're kissing her feet and making her giggle, making themselves giggle. Even the dog is giggling. This moment is perfect. Perfect like a mouthful of strawberries, perfect like the clink of two champagne glasses, perfect like a call to tell you how perfect you are!
The phone is ringing—
Perfect like a wrapped present.

But she doesn't answer.
Perfect like a warm towel.
Because why would she?
Perfect like the taste of perfume on your lips after a wet summer kiss.
Why would she?
Perfect like—
She has everything she needs right here.
Perfect like a—
Perfect like—
The phone is still ringing.

SCENE NINETEEN

The oval. PB *and* ABBIE. PB*'s eating gummy bears.*

PB: Thirty-one days. Can you believe it?
ABBIE: …
PB: Abbie?
ABBIE: What?
PB: Thirty-one days left, not including weekends.
ABBIE: Oh.
PB: Gummy bear?

> ABBIE *looks at it, then shakes her head.*

So have you voted yet?
ABBIE: For what?
PB: On Alana Tang's poll?
> She's asking people what shoes they think she should wear to 'Kieran's pre-exam party'. A new pair of Nikes or a new pair of Reeboks. Sixteen people have voted Nikes, fourteen people have voted Reeboks. It's a tough one. It's like, what are you going for? Comfort, style or statement? It's also one of those things where the shape of your leg and ankle really matters. If you've got small ankles and small feet you can get away with chunkier shoes, whereas Alana's ankles, I don't want to seem mean but—
ABBIE: Isn't it weird to know some kid, probably the same age as us, living on the other side of the world, makes our shoes.

> *Slight beat.*

PB: Umm. I guess it's weird, if you think about it like *that*, it's weird.
ABBIE: They're on the other side of the world making shoes for millions of people that they don't even know, when they probably don't even get to wear the shoes themselves.
PB: Maybe they don't want to wear the shoes because it's like wearing their work. Like the same way I can't even look at a cinnamon scroll because it reminds me of working at the bakery.
ABBIE: They probably have no say in it. That's just their life. Why were they chosen to do it?
PB: I dunno.
ABBIE: Why do they have to sit in a warehouse all day?
PB: I dunno.
ABBIE: Why does the rest of the world get to walk around in the shoes that they've made?
PB: I dunno. I still don't even know if I'm going to vote Nikes or Reeboks.
ABBIE: Are you even listening to me?
PB: Yes!
ABBIE: Who cares?
PB: It's just something to do. Are you okay?
ABBIE: Yes.
PB: Are you sure?
ABBIE: I'm awesome.
PB: Okay. Well … I'm voting Reeboks.

SCENE TWENTY

Lachie's room. ABBIE *and* LACHIE.

ABBIE: His room is smaller than I imagined. I sit on the edge of his bed chewing gum that I've had in my mouth since lunch. It's making me feel sick but it's worth it for fresh breath.
LACHIE: Do you need a drink or a tissue or—?
ABBIE: I can tell he's nervous. He keeps running his hand through his hair while he rearranges random objects around the room as if he's tidying up. We talk for a bit, about dumb things, school mostly but I didn't come here to complain about exams so as soon as there's a lull in conversation, I launch my face into his. Probably a little

too forcefully. Our teeth clink, then my nose goes into his eye for a second but he doesn't care and neither do I. We fall back to the head of his bed—

LACHIE: I'll leave the blind open so I can keep an eye on the driveway.

ABBIE: His parents aren't due home for another two hours but he's right, it's good to be safe. I press my hands into his chest and crawl on top. My hips press into his, my knees sink into the bed either side of him. He's skinnier than I expected, maybe even skinnier than me. It feels like I could crush him with my thighs if I tried.

I don't.

We kiss for what feels like forever. I feel like I'm in a movie, except I'm using all my strength not to scratch the shit out of my nipples. Everyone tells you how sexy lace is, but no-one tells you how itchy it is.

LACHIE: You have really soft skin.

ABBIE: His hands are cold and clammy. When he touches my stomach, it sends a shiver down my spine. The stomach is surprisingly intimate. I don't really know what to do so I just bite him on the neck around his ear. Finally, his hands have found their way to my—

LACHIE: Nice bra.

ABBIE: He's squeezing my boobs like they're sponges. It's weird but it kind of relieves the itch.

LACHIE: You still want to do this?

ABBIE nods enthusiastically.

ABBIE: I wouldn't be here if I didn't. In sync, we quickly undress. He has a sort of gross desperation on his face, I'm not sure what's on mine.

We start kissing again but this time it's faster and messier and I've ended up underneath. His breath is kind of hot on my neck. His hands crawl down my body and then his fingernail clips the top of my scar. I look up at the ceiling. It's covered in glow-in-the-dark spaceship stickers. I can feel his leg hair on mine, I start to wrap my legs around his back when—

He finishes.

LACHIE: Sorry.
ABBIE: It's over.
LACHIE: Sorry that was so—

ABBIE: Quick.
LACHIE: Sorry I couldn't—
ABBIE: That was it? That was more underwhelming than a canteen sausage roll. He starts reaching for a tissue when—
LACHIE: It's good to know that you can't get pregnant, but maybe I'll last longer next time if I wear a—
ABBIE: Shit. Shit. And instantly I feel like shit.

SCENE TWENTY-ONE

ABBIE *is crouched behind a bush.* PB *enters surreptitiously with a grocery bag and crouches with* ABBIE.

PB: I have them.
ABBIE: *Extra large?*
PB: You know it.
ABBIE: Twelve or—
PB: Twenty-four.
ABBIE: Good.
PB: I figured the more the better.
ABBIE: Anyone see you?
PB: Nup.

    ABBIE *looks in the bag.*

ABBIE: You got *caged*?
PB: Yeah … ?
ABBIE: That's fucked.
PB: We're not *eating* them.
ABBIE: Doesn't matter.
PB: Free-range was like *triple* the price. And I read that half of those eggs that claim to be free range are not even free range.
    Now, which is his?
ABBIE: BMW.
PB: Of course it is! Entitled [*yelling*] DICK!!
ABBIE: Shh! We're trying to keep a low profile.
PB: [*whispering*] Sorry, sorry.
ABBIE: Okay, so when the path's clear we just run out and go for it, throw as many as we can before someone sees.

PB: Or, we could casually walk up to the car, like we're just checking it out and just slowly crush eggs all over it.
ABBIE: But if we get seen we won't do much damage. We want maximum damage, shortest amount of time.
PB: Great! Run and bomb it is.

    ABBIE *hands* PB *a cut-up pair of stockings to act as a balaclava.*

ABBIE: Put this on.
PB: Oh my God. This is hilarious.
ABBIE: Why?
PB: Is this a real balaclava?
ABBIE: It's just one of my mum's old stockings.
PB: Wait, have you set me up? Are we actually about to rob a bank?
ABBIE: What?
PB: Just joking. Is egging even a crime?
ABBIE: I guess it's considered vandalism.
PB: So we'd be vandals?
ABBIE: We're not vandals.
PB: What do you reckon would actually happen if we got caught?
ABBIE: Nothing.
PB: We'd get a warning, right? It wouldn't go on our permanent record or anything, would it?
ABBIE: We really don't need to overthink this.
PB: I'm just saying it wouldn't haunt us later.
ABBIE: Maybe if you wanted to become a lawyer or a judge.
PB: [*concerned*] Really?
ABBIE: It's not going to haunt us. Boys do this stuff all the time.

    ABBIE *takes out a drink bottle and sculls a bit.*

Do you think Will and Pez thought about pissing down the C Block stairs before they did it?

    ABBIE *hands the bottle to* PB. PB *drinks and then spits it out.*

Don't waste it!
PB: Since when do you carry vodka?
ABBIE: It's gin.
PB: Since when do you carry gin? You hate gin.

ABBIE: I just thought it'd make this more fun. I can do it by myself if you're too—
PB: Abbie are you—
ABBIE: What?
PB: What exactly did Lachie do?
ABBIE: I told you.
PB: What did Lachie do to you?
ABBIE: *I told you.*
PB: You just said—
ABBIE: I said he was a dick.
PB: But did he *do* something to you?
ABBIE: He was a dick. Okay. Can't that be enough?
PB: Of course.
ABBIE: If you don't want to do this—
PB: What?
ABBIE: I can do this on my own if you're not—
PB: No. I'm here.

PB takes the bottle and sculls the drink then makes a gag face.

Let's do it.
ABBIE: Okay. Well, I think now is our moment.
PB: NOW IS OUR MOMENT! This is our moment in time.
ABBIE: I mean, no-one's around …
PB: Oh yeah.
ABBIE: If anyone sees us, we run in opposite directions and then meet at the back of Maccas carpark. Okay?

PB nods.

Okay. Three, two, one. Go!

ABBIE and PB pull the stockings over their faces and run out screaming, like a war cry. They throw eggs against the car together. The eggs from the outside look real but when they crack red dust should explode out. ABBIE pulls away from the egging while PB continues. The crackling static of electricity builds. PB eventually disappears. ABBIE is left alone.

SCENE TWENTY-TWO

The 'not-quite-real' world. ABBIE *stands in a plume of smoke.*

ABBIE: Just as they were before. Her cheeks are flushed. No. Blushed. Her face is blushed and the phone is still ringing. She looks to the man, brushes the crumbs off his lip, tucks his hair behind his ear and kisses him on the cheek. He pulls away. She doesn't notice. She does. She doesn't. She's distracted. She's distracted by the day. Distracted by the *beautiful* day. Distracted by the hard yellow crust forming around the soft melted cheese. By the lipstick-stained champagne. So she takes a sip. The bubbles turn to splinters in her throat. The dog starts barking and the bundle starts to scream. She tells them to *shoosh*. To stop that noise. There's nothing to scream about. She reaches for the child. But it sinks beneath the clumps of spoiled strawberries. A cold wind sets in. The air becomes heavy. She looks up. Her sky is black.

SCENE TWENTY-THREE

Outside school. PB *approaches* ABBIE.

PB: Where've you been?
ABBIE: The oval.
PB: For a week?
ABBIE: What?
PB: I feel like I haven't seen you in forever.
ABBIE: …
PB: What were you doing at the oval?
ABBIE: Nothing.
PB: Nothing?
ABBIE: Just didn't feel like listening to Mr Blake go on about Ophelia as a symbol of *sexualised madness* or whatever.

    PB *nods.*

PB: Well, I covered for you. I told him that you had a doctor's appointment.
ABBIE: Why would you do that?
PB: Because he was going to call the office.
ABBIE: You don't need to do that.

PB: Sorry ...
>I've got your essay.
>
>PB *hands it to* ABBIE.

ABBIE: [*surprised*] Credit?
PB: I told you to get special consideration.
ABBIE: Whatever. It's not like it even means anything.

>PB *sniffs the air around* ABBIE.

PB: You smell weird.
ABBIE: Thanks.
PB: Like cigarettes and air freshener. You smell like Cleo Bottaro.

>ABBIE *shrugs*.

ABBIE: She was at the oval.
PB: So you were smoking with Cleo Bottaro?
ABBIE: I was just sitting next to her.
PB: Watching her smoke?
ABBIE: Talking. She's actually pretty funny.
PB: Yeah, she seems like she'd be funny.
ABBIE: She is.

>*Awkward beat.*

PB: Cool. Well—
ABBIE: I can't hang tonight.
PB: Neither.
ABBIE: What are *you* doing?
PB: Mum's actually planned this big family dinner, she's cooking and everything.
ABBIE: Your mum doesn't cook.
PB: I know.
ABBIE: Is she getting married again?
PB: No! Well, I hope not!
ABBIE: So why is she having this big family dinner?
PB: ... For me, actually. I got this thing, this cadetship thing with this law firm. She's cooking dinner to celebrate. It's probably going to be terrible and we'll just end up ordering pizza.
ABBIE: You got a cadetship?
PB: Yeah.

ABBIE: When?

PB: Mrs Dougherty told me last week.

ABBIE: Last week?

PB: I forgot that she'd even given it to me. She quickly ushered me into her office, I actually thought she was going to yell at me for egging Lachie's car and then she gave me the letter, talked about my debating and then was like *'Okay, bye, you've got a practice exam in ten minutes.'*

ABBIE: Why didn't you tell me?

PB: I ... forgot.

ABBIE: So what does it mean?

PB: Basically I'm like their sponsor child. And I like *grow* with them, it's a probation thing, like I obviously have to get good marks but if I don't totally fuck it up, then it'll be a part time job while I'm at uni.

... It's probably just getting coffees, like they probably do it as a tax cut.

You should come. Come to dinner at mine.

ABBIE: I dunno.

PB: You should totally come!

ABBIE: I don't want to impose on family dinner.

PB: I always impose on your family dinners.

ABBIE: You're like my mum's second child. Your mum already has five kids, she doesn't need me.

PB: She probably wouldn't even notice.

ABBIE: I probably should just go home.

PB: Come! Seven o'clock.

ABBIE: Maybe.

PB: Okay. Well, don't forget we're going to Kieran's party together.

ABBIE: Yeah.

SCENE TWENTY-FOUR

ABBIE *is alone getting ready for the party. She's got the same drink bottle from when she egged Lachie's car and she takes swigs of gin throughout the scene.*

PB *is also getting ready alone, in her room.* PB *messages Abbie.*

ABBIE *ignores the messages.*

Text messages: all in separate texts and a buzz with each new message.

PB: *What time are we going to Kieran's?*

PB: *[Clock emoji]*

PB: *Do you wanna come to mine?*

PB: *I have chocolate and Malibu under my bed.*

> Malibu can be changed to an alcoholic drink relevant to young people.

PB: *[Party Emoji]*

PB: *But if you want I can come to yours?*

PB: *Do you still have that bottle of gin?*

PB: *I also hid some gummy bears behind your desk.*

PB: *We could have gin gummy bears or whatever they are.*

PB: *How should we get there?*

PB: *Maybe your mum could drive us?*

PB: *Or should we train?*

PB: *Or maybe I won't drink and I can drive.*

PB: *Public transport is shit.*

PB: *And I have netball tomorrow.*

PB: *Also if I drive we can get McFlurrys on the way home.*

PB: *[Ice-cream emojis]*

PB: *DONE.*

PB: *Abbieeee?*

PB: *Where are you?*

PB: *What's going on?*

PB *calls.*

ABBIE *doesn't answer.*

PB *calls again.*

ABBIE *doesn't answer.*

PB: *Answer me.*

SCENE TWENTY-FIVE

Kieran's party. The thunder is mixed in with the low drone of house music. It's smoky.

ABBIE *has turned up alone.*

ABBIE: Everything's spinning. I hear it before I see it.

Small beat.

I follow the fairy lights around the back. I run my hand along the side of the house, crouching under the trees to avoid the spiderwebs. I'd forgotten how unsettling the entrance to a party is. I quickly scout the yard for a group to join but everyone's in the dark. I buy myself time. Plunge my hand deep into the esky. The ice burns my skin. I clutch a can of something and pull it out like a lucky dip. The bubbles burn my throat and make my eyes water. I like that feeling almost as much as I like the way the plastic of the upturned crate digs into my thighs when I sit down next to Kevin.

KEVIN: Jack Daniels'. Nice. Cheers.

They cheers.

You like bourbon?

ABBIE: Not really.

KEVIN: That's why I drink alcoholic ginger beer. Tastes exactly like regular ginger beer only it's alcoholic. I give it four out of five stars.

Do you wanna try some?

ABBIE: Not really.

KEVIN: Fair. I sometimes get cold sores. I don't have one now, but you know, you never know. So, you thought about what you're gonna do when we finish?

Abbie's phone buzzes.

ABBIE: Nope.

KEVIN: Really? No plans?

ABBIE: I haven't really thought about it.

KEVIN: Yeah, me neither.

Abbie's phone buzzes.

KEVIN *starts nodding his head to the music.*

    You like this music?

ABBIE: Not really.

KEVIN: What sort of music do you like?

Abbie's phone buzzes and the soft crackling of electricity and thunder start to grow.

ABBIE: I don't know.

KEVIN: C'mon. You have to know what music you like.

ABBIE *begins to dissociate from Kevin and the party.*

ABBIE: They're sitting on a polka dot picnic blanket.

KEVIN: You don't speak very much.

ABBIE: The three of them.

KEVIN: It's kind of disconcerting.

ABBIE: Under the dappled sunlight of a tree.

KEVIN: When you don't speak—

ABBIE: Their very own Garden of Eden.

KEVIN: It's hard to know what you're thinking—

ABBIE *snaps back.*

ABBIE: Why would you want to know that?

KEVIN: Sorry, I was just—

ABBIE: She runs.

SCENE TWENTY-SIX

The 'not-quite-real' world. ABBIE *is completely encased in fog and ash-like spores. The crackling of electricity and the groan of thunder grow around her. It gets more intense as it goes.*

ABBIE: It strikes.
    The wind.
    It whips at her heels.
    And pounds in her head.
    She can't look back.
    The ground cracks around her.
    She can't look back.
    She stumbles.

The echo.
Gets louder.
She feels it.
All over.
She can't look back.
She closes her eyes.
It's still there.
The whole world on top of her.

> *From the shadows.*

PB: Abbie … ?
ABBIE: The whole world.
PB: ABBIE?

SCENE TWENTY-SEVEN

A park. ABBIE *is sitting on a swing. Headlights come towards her. A figure comes out of the darkness. It's* PB.

PB: What the fuck is going on?
   Kevin told me you ran out.
   I've been texting you.

> ABBIE *doesn't respond.*

PB: *Nothing?*
   You're not going to say anything?
   Just going to pretend I'm not here?

> *Abbie's phone starts to ring. She doesn't answer it.*

PB: Do you wanna answer that?
ABBIE: I can decide whether I want to answer my own phone or not.

> *It keeps ringing.*

PB: It's probably your mum.
ABBIE: I'm not an idiot.
PB: She's driving around looking for you.
ABBIE: How would you know that?
PB: Because we were worried about you!

> *PB's phone starts ringing, she goes to answer it—*

ABBIE: Don't answer it.
>If you answer that phone, I'll never speak to you again.

>PB *lets the phone ring out.*

ABBIE: Why are you looking at me like that?
PB: Like what?!
ABBIE: Like one wrong move and I'll break.
PB: What the fuck are you talking about?
ABBIE: I'm strong. I'm stronger than all of you. So you can stop feeling sorry for me. You and everyone else can STOP feeling SO SORRY FOR ME—
PB: I'm not like everyone else and I don't feel sorry for you!
Or maybe I do.
I don't know!
I don't know what to do or say or not do or not say.
What you're going through is shit and no-one knows how to deal with it, no-one knows how to deal with anything.
I don't know how you're feeling?! Are you pissed off? Are you hurt? Are you relieved? What can I do? Tell me what to do!
Do you want to buy cheap plates from Kmart and throw them at the soccer wall? Do you want to shoplift from Coles? Egg some more cars? Sneak into a club? Whatever! Just tell me.
I'm sorry that this has happened to you but stop pushing me away because you think I don't understand or because you think you don't deserve my help or whatever self-pitying shit you're telling yourself.
You're my best friend.
I love you.

>*She gets nothing.*

But if you don't want me around anymore, just say it.

>PB *goes towards* ABBIE. ABBIE *pushes* PB *back. It shocks them both.*

ABBIE: Leave me alone.
PB: Abbie …

>PB*'s gone.*

SCENE TWENTY-EIGHT

The 'not-quite-real' world. ABBIE *is alone. The storm is all around her.*

ABBIE: The sky is black.
    The light has gone.
    The Garden of Eden
    The light has gone.
    The polka dot picnic blanket.
    The light has gone.
    She closes her eyes
    She covers her ears.
    The sound gets louder.
    It's closing in.
    Her breath …
    She can't—
MUM: Where've you been?
ABBIE: Mum?
MUM: Thank God you're alright.
ABBIE: MUM.

SCENE TWENTY-NINE

Abbie's house. Night.

MUM: What's going on?
ABBIE: My throat feels lumpy so I don't answer.
MUM: Abbie—
ABBIE: I brush past.
MUM: Abbie! Don't ignore me.
ABBIE: I stop but don't turn around.
MUM: I know it must be lonely.
ABBIE: She walks up behind me.
MUM: But everyone is trying their best.
ABBIE: I feel like I can't breathe.
MUM: Everyone is trying their best with what they have.
ABBIE: My eyes are stinging but I hold it in.

MUM: It's easy to hurt others when you're hurting.
ABBIE: I want to pull away but I'm stuck.
MUM: I'm so proud of who you are.
ABBIE: It starts to come.
MUM: We love you so much.
ABBIE: Hot tears in my mouth.
MUM: You are so *so* loved.

>ABBIE *lets go. She lets go of all of it.*
>
>*She collapses into* MUM*'s chest and sobs and sobs and sobs until there's nothing left.*
>
>*A long moment of silence.*

SCENE THIRTY

The 'not-quite-real' world. This time there is no fog. No spores. The storm has passed. The world is warm.

ABBIE: There she is. Under the dappled sunlight of a tree. Where she was before. Not sitting, but standing. She walks up to the empty polka dot picnic blanket. She has one last look around before rolling it up and walking away.

SCENE THIRTY-ONE

School hall. Formal. Low beats of a school dance and disco lights.

PB *stands there in the corner of the room, alone, no coat.*

Not long after, ABBIE *arrives wearing her giant fur coat.*

They catch each other's eye.

ABBIE *stops and then decides to walk up to* PB.

There's a distance between them.

ABBIE: Hey.
PB: Hey.

>*Awkward silence.*

ABBIE: Have you seen Mr Lee yet?
PB: No.

ABBIE: He was doing the worm and then threw his back out.
PB: Oh.

> *Another silence.*

ABBIE: And Caitlin Gregg brought her pet rat. It's in the top pocket of her jacket.
PB: I saw.
ABBIE: Isn't that animal cruelty or something?
PB: Probably.

> *Small pause.*

I didn't think you were going to wear it.
ABBIE: Last-minute decision.
PB: Aren't you *sweating your tits off?*
ABBIE: Beauty is pain.

> *A moment.*

I'm sorry.

> PB *is quiet.*

I'm really sorry that I hurt you.

> *It hangs.*

> ABBIE *takes out a packet of gummy bears and offers them to* PB.

> PB *looks at them for a moment and then walks away.*

> ABBIE *stands there alone.*

> *It feels long and awkward.*

> PB *returns wearing the fur coat and sunglasses and walks up to* ABBIE.

PB: I read somewhere, probably the internet and probably from an unreliable source that human touch relieves anger and pain. So—

> PB *opens her arm for a hug.*

> ABBIE *takes a second before launching at* PB. *They hug tightly.*

> *It's tender.*

I've missed you.
ABBIE: Me too.

PB takes the gummy bears and excitedly stretches, the way runners nervously stretch just before the beginning of a race.

PB: So what's our game plan?

ABBIE: I think we start at the front, then as we go, we slowly drop back to where there's more room for bigger dance moves.

PB: Go hard or go home.

ABBIE: We're undeniable.

PB: We're unstoppable.

ABBIE: And we're never going to see these fuckers again.

PB nods.

PB: Alright.

ABBIE: Alright. Ready?

PB: Ready.

ABBIE and PB look at each other and then link arms.

They turn to face the dance floor. They're ready.

They walk closer. The music swells louder.

Just as the beat drops—blackout.

THE END